PERPENDICULAR

Perpendicular

By

Shirley Olive Sam

ISBN: 978-1-961677-84-5 (Paperback)

Printed in the United States of America

Published by

info@thequippyquill.com
(302) 295-2278

Contents

Papa's Angel

If I were a little taller
I could reach up to the sky
I will touch all the tall buildings
Handglide down the mountains, too

All the people who will hurt me
I can tell them from up here
You can't touch me--you can't see me
I think I am invisible

I see mama and papa crying
Why did my child disappear
What does a sweet engaging angel
Run away from--I just can't see

How painful your life must have been
To create such an emergency
My child, my child, I did not know
Forgive me munchkin, papa tried

His best to give--always loving you
I wish that I had told you sooner
You could have stayed--not run away
I hope you will come back someday

My dear Papa--I miss you so
From up here I can see you, though
Your memories now will have to suffice
See I was hit not once--but twice

Copyright, 2023 Shirley Sam

Renewal

No need to cry--no need for sorrow
Nor head bowed down in misery
The angels--can't you hear the singing
Can't you discern the bells, the harps
The ringing chorus loud and sharp

Picture for a little while yet
The cloudless sky, the moonlit night
The thousand voices singing softly
Loudly as the rhapsody
Melodious, chanting, lifting o'er us

Taking us to places unknown
Blotting out four seasons gone
Teasing, luring, willing us on
Forgetting hard times, there's only here and now
We cannot resist we'll relish always
The beautiful, the here and now

Majestic and bountiful music
Fills the air and heads held high
We celebrate life, we taste and feel it
Another year of cares has gone
We take the time to share we give it
Another magnanimous try free

With heartfelt thundering we express it
We promise ourselves a better year
When once again we come together
To reaffirm each other here
That in this place--right here and now
We will partake--renew our vow

Copyright, 2023 Shirley Sam

Faith

Funny how we seem to grow
Stronger with each glancing blow
The anvil does its best and yet
We seem to weather every set
Of rigors, storms, adversity

We do not readily submit
We never, ever say "I quit"
How then do we survive it all
And keep on smiling through it all
We know no other way to get
To the other side, except get wet

How does it work, how can we smile
While others perish at every mile
The road is covered with the lot
Of others lost along the way
They struggled for a while and then
Because they could not see the end

The rainbow has elusive been
The pottage, rationed has all gone
The victors, weary and disheveled
Have crossed the road, regained their lead
And exit smiling as the race

Continues for the few, the brave
Who conquered all their fears, and now
Shine forth with great aplomb and grace
And name the main ingredient—Faith

Copyright, 2023 Shirley Sam

Intro to my Art

I must have read somewhere that art equals pain: reworked, revised improved upon, but pain nonetheless. A means of expressing the anguish and innermost joy or fury of the one so impoverished. The perpetual flowing from a seemingly endless source of pathos.

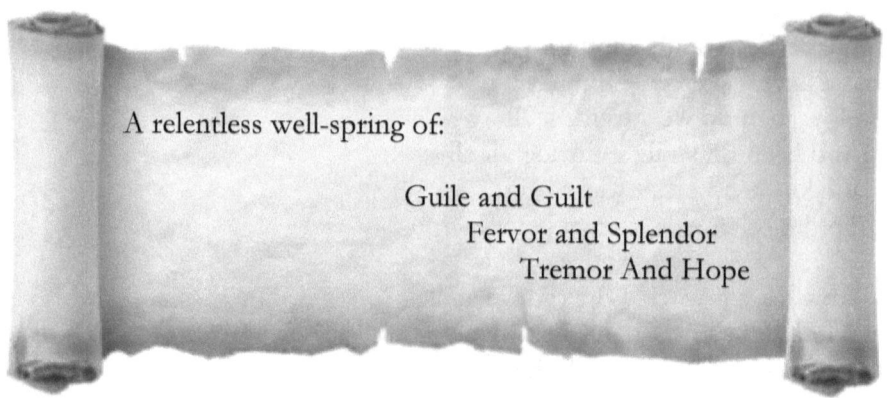

A relentless well-spring of:

Guile and Guilt
Fervor and Splendor
Tremor And Hope

A truly cleansing and uplifting experience.
If poetry can be considered art, then I offer my art for your perusal and publication.

Foreword to   **"The Olive Branch Series"**

Authored By   **Shirley Olive Dorothy Sam**   **S.O.S**

RESTRAINTS- CHAINS

From chains I struggled to break free
Their origin was a mystery to me
My crime if so it can be called, was to be born into this world

Unshackled I will like to be
Not wrestling in this misery
My bonds restrict my human form, they cannot touch my inner norm

Sometimes I'm tempted to give in, my mortal self says why not - then
That inner voice that will not quit
Reproves the whole and calms again

My beleaguered soul seeks to inquire
What have I done that was so dire
Does this package redeem itself; or wantonly, dangerously, cling to a shelf

My severed moorings to repair, go on from here to who knows where
Regain composure perhaps attain, the goal I sought ere this all began
Such things I cannot contemplate not while I'm wallowing in my fate

I do not choose to emerge from here until my place in this world is clear
And I can see with all clarity the writing on the wall for me
You have a perfect guarantee...

That life will never let you down
Because you are the greatest--this to the wise would cause upset
Cause man was never meant to be

Macabre in his integrity
To strive, to purpose, to attain this is the great agenda--the same
Of life was meant for you, for me

To echo those of long ago, who came, and saw, and worked to gain
A place in history and fame, and hills will tell with sweet recall
When faced with troubles, against the wall
You struggled always to impart

The greatest love that you could give
To one and all; with might and mien your treasured moments, precious
life
Is to keep trying-- come what may you just might win another day

The chains are broken- I am free
My offspring will inspired be
For right and wrong the coin is tossed who will suffer so great a loss

If this lesson does not impart my joy, my sorrow, and my heart

Copyright 2023   "The Olive Branch Series"

Authored By   Shirley Olive Dorothy Sam   S.O.S

Lonesome One

You wondered off so long ago
"I will return, I need to go"
Your parting words, as you left that day
You did return, to tears and sorrow
But not as promised, on the morrow

Your parents, they have long since gone
They wanted for you to come home
Your friends have traveled o'er the realm
So why did you not hear the call
Or see the writing on the wall

Significant other aside
So tell me, was it worth the price
The lofty expectations--all
Have long evaporated--gone
And now perish here alone
Take comfort, solace, lonesome one

The stars, they will come out again
The sun will rise, as you well ken
Your hopes, your dreams, they will revive
You have returned, you will survive
Child of the universe you are
You rally round your guiding star

Courage

Forgive me child, I have been wrong
I wondered--could you carry on
Many a time you seemed so lost
I imagined could you pay the cost
You seemed so forlorn and alone
I hoped you could find your way home

My image of you I couldn't ignore
You always seemed to pound on closed doors
No longer satisfied are you
To hobble over slippery stones
And limp along on broken bones

The challenge you have met and then
Gone on to be a champion
The wrinkled, worried brow once knit
Now smoothed; anticipate your gift
To a waiting world, you did not quit

You carried on with might and mien
Although you faltered, trembled, too
Your faith, hope, life and courage true
Stood you in good stead--for you know
That someone, somewhere, believed in you

My Angel Child

My angel child I search for you
I'm told you're gone--no need for me
To wait and wonder where you are
You're gone just like a shooting star

Sometimes at night I sit and wonder
What might have been if you had stayed
Would you handle your situation
Any differently--would you have played

The saxophone, the trumpet even
What instrument would you have been
What rationale would then be given
Would have been you my wunderkind

My angel child--too soon you left us
We'll never know what might have been
Too soon the clouds enveloped you
Took you away from us--and then

A child is lost--too soon forgotten
A life is shattered--too soon spent
The world has seen to his demise
The milk of human kindness never

Nurtured of cherished this infant
He sees his boundaries, limits even
As the playground he never knew
Would that the clock would travel backward

We would receive a second chance
If only to reward his suffering
With generous, loving, helping hands

Self

The questioning goes on and on
Pray tell--who is the curmudgeon
Which one of us is first to quit
Or do we continue to spit

Venom clear across the room
Where once there was such harmony
Have we welcomed our own doom
Subconsciously, unwittingly
Sealed our own fate, revived the gloom

We seldom see each other now
We hang in there, consoled somehow
By earlier joys which we're denied
Because of our own stubborn pride
Which won't let go of slights and hide
Again behind our foolish pride

It's over now, the battle's done
I see no victor, who has won
When all is said and done you see
It all comes down to you and me
If our daily problems we can't resolve

How can we possibly evolve
To a higher plain of ecstasy
We're self-destructive--you and me

Force Field

I'm an enigma I've been told
By acquaintances who try to fold
And package me into a mold
Of their own making

As a friend you are priceless
As a human being--you are divine
To those who know you, or think they do
You are an energetic force field
In the making

Of bands of gold you reign supreme
Of jeweled lights you are la creme
You nurture, you cherish, you create anew
A force field one cannot subdue

To know you friend is to perceive
To see the world as a reprieve
From blades of grass to strands of gold
From icy glades to prisms pure
Your love of nature will endure

Copyright, 2023 Shirley Sam

MAMA--- WHEN CAN I SING

MY sisters all, my brothers too
Have gone on to seek their fortune
They hover near the glitter dome
They never seem to enter

The keys they need they don't possess
The love and joy they cherish
They only see the other side
They never seem to enter

Into that spotlight they would wade
If only they could enter in
So long temerity-- here I come
With all the others I will join
In singing and remembering

The days, the years of waiting
Just to sing along with glee
Must have taught me to be humble
To learn to appreciate fully

The brotherhood, the togetherness
The savoir faire, the repertoire
All culminating in ever-changing scenes
To reach the clouds, the heavens and then
Reverberate and back again

Perhaps someone else's life to enrich
Find fertile ground in which to grow
To ever new, stupendous heights
Surpass our wildest, grandest dreams

Someone to bless and in so doing
Make lives worthwhile, that is our hope
For somebody to learn to cope
With life's many trials, great and small
Forever changed---God bless us all

Copyright 2023   **" The Olive Branch Series"**

Authored By   **Shirley Olive Dorothy Sam**   **S.O.S**

PERPENDICULAR

1. A NEW DANGER
2. A RAINY DAY
3. BEGUILED
4. CHAINS"
5. COURAGE
6. DIAMOND
7. ESPERANZA
8. FAITH
9. FORCE FIELD
10. FUN
11. GIFTS OF LOVE
12. GOLDEN YEARS
13. HAPPY HEARTS
14. I GRIEVE ALONE
15. LOVERS-PREDESTINED
16. LONESOME ONE
17. LIVING GHOSTS
18. MAMA, WHEN CAN I SING
19. MY ANGEL CHILD
20. MY REVERIE
21. O, CHILD O MIINE
22. PAPA'S ANGEL
23. REMEMBERING
24. RENEWAL
25. RHAPSODY
26. ROLLING HILLS
27. SELF
28. STARS
29. TO PEACE-HARMONY
30. TO CLAIM HIS CROWN
31. PERPENDICULAR
32. BIRDS…THE WINDOWSILL

A New Danger

A little plant opened up down the road
How can a plant look like a building
What's open up and where is down
I think they are confusing me

Our neighbors say it is no good
Shouldn't be in this neighborhood
What can we do, who can we see
To take this plant away and leave

It makes me very sad to see
This nice gentle man who can't see
Complain of things both then and now
How they have changed, kaboom, kapow

We saw the wars, we fought there, too
How come we can't even say boo
Nobody listens then or now
Somehow I think we've unseen now

The war's been fought, the victory's won
We've outdone ourselves, so how come now
Nobody listens, our voices raised
We get nowhere except we say
We'll come again another day

Esperanza

Enter pain, enter despair
You travel far to reach me
Now I may choose to vacillate
I cannot entertain you here
Though fate conspires to entrap

Engulf me with a world of care
I seek to free myself and yet
Unknown to me I am bereft
Of outstretched arms, a world of love
My comfort zone

Enter the light that banishes
The dreaded gloom, hello wishes
And hope, and trust, and shining ray
 Illuminate my world and say

Though troubled for a little while
It will return--your own sweet smile
With passions burning, zest and zeal
Grace to the world you will reveal

For you are Chosen, you will be
Forever smiling, hoping, free
The price already has been paid
You cannot help but face the gale
And then triumphantly declare
Faith, hope, charity," Esperanza"

Copyright, 2023 Shirley Sam

Fun

They meet as friends then as lovers
A teenage couple wide-eyed and young
They roam the craggy streets together
And find courage amid the throng

Of displaced persons like themselves
Who rove and desperately try
To finagle or borrow even
A smile, a frown, a wandering eye
Someone to say please do not cry

Will there ever be song and dance
How do we emerge from this trance
Of self-imposed restrictions--now
That we have left it all behind
We won't return--we made a vow

To see each other through it all
We didn't know that we could fall
Through nooks and crannies in the wall
Of this fabric of society
That will not help us--how could we

Have seen and known that this our life
Will be over so soon--we've hardly begun
To live, to experience it all
We need to breath, to live, have fun

Gifts of Love

God gave us each a little care
A little pain we have to bear
We sometimes wish it were different
Yet still we know that were it so
We couldn't conquer even then

Ourselves alone the grief we carry
Would weigh us down--no cross, no crown
So humbly we ask for grace to bear
Each passing day we do our share
And gratefully accept the challenge

Of daily care and joy and sorrow
It will be better on the morrow
How do we know if not first hand
That we will be better humans
And treat each other with regard

Respect for all, we expect, we give
For a better world in which to live
Our children s' offspring will enjoy
With laughter and a sunny smile
We paid as others did before us

That their world will be a great chorus
Of song, peace, hope, a celebration
So rich a world--why should they suffer
The pangs of hunger, guilt, or shame

They know not from where such things came
As elders we try to ensure
Their world with all conveniences
Should be a treasure, not a burden

A Rainy Day

Splitter, splatter here it comes
Sometimes bountiful, or sparse
Still it pours and drenches maybe
The plants, the earth, or you and me

I see the rainbow shining through
The vivid colors, they inspire
A song, a rhyme, a step or two
My skin is wet, my heart afire

With burning zeal, I seek, I find
The embers playing in my mind
My soul, my heart, we welcome you
O precious outpouring of dew

The world's washed clean and bright and shiny
Shimmering like a brand new penny
A dazzling sight, only a few
Are privileged as me, as you

To greet the world, rejoice anew
To warm ourselves, and then adieu
Perhaps I grow, perhaps I dream
Relate to some, relive the scene
The beauty of what we have seen

Beguiled

Beguiled sometimes by this world's offerings
We strive in vain for wealth untold
We tarry here, we seem forlorn
We garner not, we battle always
The gold eludes us all

Wishing upon a star might soothe
And hopeful yet we carry on
We wonder still how could this happen
We paid our dues so what went wrong

The race is not to the summit
I'm told But perseverance will uphold
And strengthen, encourage us all
To run the race e'en though we fall

So many times we will ourselves
Against the strong persuasive call
Of giving in for just a taste
A respite from the bitter gall

Our lives wear on, we struggle till
With bated breath we wait
To hear the call, "Well done, my friend
You worked, you conquered, you endured
Beguiling factors are worn down
You've superseded, you have won"

Copyright, 2023 Shirley Sam

O, Child of Mine

The peacock's run--the rabbits wren
The robin's perch--the lion's den
To each of these a home is given
Pray tell--why do I ride the mizzen?

To each one an appointed place
Regardless of our creed or race
Do we endeavor, seek to find
A favorite place--o, child of mine?

The dewy, misty eyes grow dim
The things of yore--have long since been
Replaced by more sophisticated means
O, child of mine--where have I been?

Why didn't I see the ship's distant sail
Why did I not hear the siren's wail
Could I have gone so far away?
It seemed like only yesterday

My reverie--my longing spent
I now return to circumvent
My journey homeward--I must delay
To see my child another day

Copyright, 2023 Shirley Sam

My Reverie

The sun, the moon, the stars that shine
Combine to make my world divine
My spirits soar, I am imbued
By these great gifts, I am renewed

Consolation and joy they bring
They make my world a living thing
In darkest moments of despair
Within my soul I know they're there

This thirsting, hungering of mine
Will be appeased--all in good time
My sorrows and my joys commingle
Though dormant they can paint my day

In hues of green, red, blue, and yellow
Color my universe supreme
Iridescent in shades that mellow
That meld and mesh and subtly scream

Surprising in their raucous splendor
They sing, they dance, they jump with glee
Cavorting, flitting, splashing always
My world, my treasures though unseen
By others, they will always be
My niche, my home, my reverie

Stars

Majestic skies of cobalt blue
For this my heart is yearning
When last I looked upon your face
The stars seemed to be burning

With purity they danced and played
They skipped amid the clover
Though now they seem forever gone
Alas they died aborning

When first I saw their lovely gaze
They seemed like pearls adorning
The heavens, the Milky Way, the streams
Of silver threads upon the maze

The rivulets of gloss and glitter
Twinkling far away, yet seemingly
So near, so close, so very close
That touching them would only serve

The wishful longing to preserve
And fantasies then will abound
That lovers, friends, and family, too
Could ride the Milky Way and see
Forever yonder, and beyond
The veil, the curtain, a distant land

Copyright, 2023 Shirley Sam

To Claim His Crown

We surface now, we have been gone
For quite some time we've tried to say
To seek your own deserved crown
You work out your own destiny

And now with new exuberance
on We sally forth with glee
We sought, we found, and we pressed on
To our own destiny

We cherish now our dreams anew
We diligently seek the shore
Where for a jester and a clown
Our sage old grandpa left his home
To find that one spark, his own crown

Ere he departs this weary frame
He can now claim with utmost pride
"I've seen the hills, I've seen the valleys
I do not want or need to hide"

With head held high, I can declare
I've seen it all, I've done it all
I can return from whence I came
Tis hail, farewell, and then begone
I'll claim my well-deserved crown

To Peace-Harmony

The sun's rays shine
In a spectacular unfurling
Of burnt orange, gold, brown, and every hue
As they sit upon the horizon

The glowing embers are laid to rest
Another day is done and yet
So smoothly, calmly, should the cares
Now dissipate, dissolve away
And enter peace--sweet harmony
We've survived yet another day

Tis done, tis done, the eagle's cry
A with weary wings so silently
Yet patiently, persistently
They wend their way inevitably
To the distant shore where they could see
Their home, sweet home, and family

To peace, sweet peace--a gift untold
Magnificent in sur-cease
A unified and gentle wafting
Of evening calm in colors bold
Unsettling in its majesty
You stand transfixed, you pause
To commit this scene to memory

Rolling Hills

From rolling hills so far away
Sounds reverberate at light of day
The rushing waters splash and quiver
Like children playing in the river

They meander and roam and splutter
The lilies, daffodils, morning glory, too
All splashed with light and sun-drenched glow
They set to work for me, for you

To make our world a happy place
Where we can roam, and skip, and gaze
With wondering eyes we seek anew
To keep the glitter of morning dew

On rosy cheeks kissed day by day
With blessings from the skies above
Where each in his own special way
Will celebrate and show his love

For the rolling hills will always be
A symbol of pure ecstasy
As they in all their grandeur stand
And welcome you with beckoning grace
Come take your fill and find your place
 You are of course, the human race

Love, Predestined

With childlike grace
She laughed and played
She sang of days gone by
She knew that there had been a time
When skies will greet you gladly

When rustling leaves would sing with you
The joy of happier times
Weep not for me, they seemed to say
My joy is hidden somehow

It will shine again! It will! It will!
Our love has been predestined
We've all seen happier times and now
Await the return of the sun

The sparkle of the moon on water
The twinkling of the cowbell's call
My home is now wherever you are
The moving train, the awesome fall
 I saw it all--so now I keen

And moan, and suffer, and yet I find
That you are with me in my waking
And sleeping hours I see your face
Our lives entwined, we once embraced
And shared a love that was predestined

Copyright, 2023 Shirley Sam

Diamond

Hello again, I've seen your face
You recognized me somehow
'Tis paler now than it was then
But you would rally somehow

Your courage speaks
Your faint heart sings
Your grace inspires volumes

Though hostile tides seem oft to swallow
You persevered then and now
You know no boundaries, you persist
In love, in hope, in sorrow

From such a course, you cannot veer
The lines are there to follow
You go the extra mile again
As diamonds glow--you sparkle

PERPENDICULAR

For as long as I can remember
I have seen these fellows go hither
They call themselves the merry few
As humans go--they are askew

Forever locked into the caste
They consider themselves outcasts
Whatever seems outrageous; they do
Perhaps you know their cousins too

The willow speaks to this genre
So softly weeping, they engender
The utmost deference of their kind
An almost worshipful incline

The willow seeks to gently guide
The solemn few within their pride
Of soulful, sorrowful and proud
They seem to grasp at that thin cloud

Of plumage radiant and rare
They hasten to renew, repair
A solemn premise as of now
The willow will in no way bow

To pressures exerted and trained
Upon the bough and round the sphere
The willow will in no wise despair
 If you should see the willow bend
You are very fortunate my friend

There are those who kinship with the willow claim
This might be their one glance at fame; surprised at their resilience
They proceed then to greater heights
Forsake the mundane; establish, their rightful place and join the fray

Hence their unusual activity ---A Perpendicular Acclivity

Copyright 2023   "The Olive Branch Series"

Authored by   Shirley Olive Dorothy Sam   S.O.S

Happy Hearts

Happy is the heart that wanders
Overdale and mountain, bog and meadow
Seeking always the hidden treasures
That can't be bought, but they are priceless
To ones redemptive spirit—values

Resurgence of a different kind
Renewing of a childlike mind
The treasure chest--the broken arrow
A child's' dreams that on the morrow
We'll ride again along the creek

Each stone a new desire brings
Where did the sea captain put his rings
How come we can't continue on
It's only night--we can't stop now
We've got to ride on to destiny

Why can't you see it over there
That's no moonlight, it is the fairy
In stories you have read to me
A little closer and you'll see
My little wigwam, my teepee
Why don't grown eyes see what I see
Did they destroy their destiny

Copyright, 2023 Shirley Sam

LIVING GHOSTS...1

The ghosts are dangling from the rafters
They're in the secret corners of my mind
Periodically they allow me laughter
My thoughts, my dreams remain sanguine

A nursery rhyme I do recall
The bough breaks and baby will fall
Into the abyss I am ensnared
You see me not, but I am there

I breathe involuntarily
I can't hold back, it's not up to me
My powers, once limitless now are
Curtailed by fear, how can I dare

Express myself without rancor
Or reprisals-- what will I incur
How heavy a price do I have to pay
To enjoy freedom-- what a day

With arms outstretched I welcome the rain
Say- can you remove every stain
Remembrances of things long past
Where did I turn, when did I lose

Myself, another to reclaim
Pray tell, what recourse do I have
When do I find the friend I lost
Where should I leave this living ghost

Portending to remove my past
My ever-present, rueful past
Should have been exorcised and yet
Around each corner, every bend

I meet my disillusioned friend
Whose memories alike as mine
Recusant, though still held in check
By a baleful, doleful hand as yet

We've suffered much with no regret
We now enjoy a curious fate
Banded together by a long-held trait
Hopefully we'll meet at Heaven's gat

Copyright 2023   **"The Olive Branch Series"**

Authored By   **Shirley Olive Dorothy Sam**   **S.O.S.**

Rhapsody

We sing a diverse melody
We languish in our misery
We reminisce of days gone by
We were so happy, you and I

Of lovers' quarrels we had a few
Somehow they were never resolved
We'd build to a crescendo—then
Fall flat, then rest, begin again

To raise the roof, propelled by
Those forces we cannot defy
That seemed to aim for greater heights
That defied even gravity

Does love have this effect on all
Its victims past and present
Or should we each erect a wall
For self-preservation and bent

On keeping our own sanity
Restrict ourselves to levity
For longing and posterity
And keenly wait for a divining
Or miracles that will set us free
A you for you and a me for me

Golden Years

Since we were young once and now
Have grown to see the perilous
The hazy side of growing up
How did we overcome and move
On to this current plateau—where

With arms outstretched we celebrate
Our entrance to the golden gate
Is all of life consistently
Agreed upon for you, for me
To age as gracefully as this
Or do we carry on with bliss

To fields afar from here we gaze
Upon the vista clear and wide
We seek to return to yesteryear
Our bodies tell us gently at first
That this our premier goal--our course
Was set a very long time ago

So hail, farewell, and auld lang syne
My friends and I we were divine
Our golden years we will enjoy
As surely as the robins fly
We will retain our dignity
E'en though we crawl upon our knees

Copyright, 2023 Shirley Sam

Remembering

My kinsmen when I think of you
Your kilted figure comes to mind
You cherished cultures have imbued
Your life with richness matching only
Your wonderfully extravagant mind

So travel softly now and speak
Lovingly of times of yore
Forgetting all the hatred, malice
The madness in settling the score

Tis done! Tis done! Better forgotten
Seek peaceful times along the shore
You play in waves as they roll by
And try to find a place of calm

Where weary souls will rest in peace
Whether on this side or the other
A wonderful and healing space
Bereft of sorrow, trials and waste

Where children can enjoy the telling
Of battles fought so long ago
And relish stories of the bogs
And soldiers coming home to rest

No more! No more! Time to move on
To build anew a life worthwhile
Resplendent and yet at once humble
A gift for one and all to see
Their fight was not in vain and yet
In remembering--we do not fret

I Grieve Alone

How come you never see me cry
When there is such a tragedy
You look for outward signs of grief
You do not see me in my pain
When longing for a kindred soul

I curl up and I want to die
But this would not my freedom bring
I carry this burden all alone
I wring my hands, I am bereft
Of solace--grief is now my kin

My years of solitude now ease
My pain, my grief I can express
In ways other than your own
My silence in no way demonstrates
The bitter agony I taste

Yet I will forsooth reveal
The origin of my ordeal
You cannot see, you'll never know
The travail I must undergo
Each time I'm called upon to say

Goodbye to someone who was loved
By others and myself and then
Was called on to another realm

Copyright, 2023 Shirley Sam

www.ingramcontent.com/pod-product-compliance
Lightning Source LLC
Chambersburg PA
CBHW020921140626
46545CB00015B/1195